THE RUSSIAN BALLET SCHOOL

Leon Harris

THE RUSSIAN BALLET SCHOOL

with photographs by the author

Atheneum 1970 New York

The author wishes to express his gratitude to Madame Ekaterina Alexeyevna Furtseva, the Minister of Culture of the U.S.S.R.; to Secretary Robert H. Finch of the Department of Health, Education, and Welfare; to Sofia Nikolaievna Golovkina, Konstantin Sergeyev, Valentin Ivanovich Shelkor, Natalia Dudinskaya, Nicolai Sharigin, E. Malachovskaya, Alexandra Dyhovicknaya, Irene Ivlieva, Alla Budrova, Vladimir Starogiloff, Victor Baturov, Yuri Bagaev, Leonid Zhdanov, Danil Saveliev, as well as all the others who were so helpful to him.

For permission to use the photographs on the title pages and on pages 2, 9, 10, 11, 32, 33, 34, 35, 36, 40, 42, 43, 44, 46, 47 right, 48, 49, 52, 53, 57, 59 the author thanks the Bolshoi School, the Kirov School and Fotokronika TASS. All other photographs are by the author.

Library of Congress catalog card number 76-115069
Published simultaneously in Canada by
McClelland and Stewart, Ltd.
Manufactured in the United States of America
Printed by The Murray Printing Company,
Forge Village, Massachusetts
Bound by H. Wolff, New York
First edition

for Dorothy Olding with love

THERE WAS BALLET IN ITALY in the fifteenth century. In the sixteenth and seventeenth centuries it was formalized in France. It did not reach Russia until the eighteenth century, but once they had discovered it, the Russians so loved ballet that they soon dominated it. From those days, through the Russian Revolution, and until today, the Russian classical ballet has been and is the best in the world.

All the great Russian composers have written for the ballet. Russian choreographers, like Michel Fokine, and impresarios, like Sergei Diaghilev, have brought to the Russian ballet the best designers (Picasso, Bakst, Derain) and the best composers (Stravinsky, Ravel, de Falla) from all over the world. But the chief glory of the Russian ballet has been and still is its dancers and these have been produced by the Russian ballet schools.

The Russian Imperial School of Ballet was founded in 1738 in the Winter Palace in St. Petersburg (now Leningrad), and has produced many of the world's greatest dancers from Pavlova and Nijinsky to Ulanova and Nureyev. It also produced such teachers, dancers, and choreographers as Egorova, Danilova, and Balanchine, who when they left Russia, because of the Revolution, brought the glory of Russian ballet to Europe and the Western Hemisphere. This school is now called the Vaganova School; but since it sends its best graduates to Leningrad's Kirov Ballet, it is often referred to as the Kirov School.

In 1773 the Moscow Orphanage began giving ballet classes to its inmates and thus started the school now known as the Moscow Ballet School. Since it supplies Moscow's Bolshoi Theatre with dancers, it is often called the Bolshoi School. These two schools, the Kirov and the

Bolshoi, are the most important, but there are eighteen other state ballet schools in the Soviet Union, as well as hundreds of amateur groups.

It has been estimated that over a million young men and women study and perform ballet in Russia on a part-time basis in various amateur clubs and factory groups, a degree of interest unmatched in any other country. Since Czarist times the ballet has represented for Russians the ultimate in glamor; and ballet stars today, both male and female, have great prestige in Russian society. Girls who have never had a ballet lesson imitate the toes-out walk

of ballet dancers as American girls might copy the hair styles or dress fashions of their favorite movie, television, or recording stars. Boys regard famous male dancers in the same way American boys look at their favorite sport heroes.

Every spring, poster and newspaper announcements explain how children may apply to take the entrance examinations for the ballet schools. Parents are very anxious for their children to go to one of them because the lives of the leading dancers in Russia are extraordinarily privileged. They are supplied free of charge by the state with the finest apartments and are so well paid that, unlike most Russians, they can afford a country home as well as servants and cars; and, of course, they travel all over the world. First-rate dancers in Russia, along with the best scientists and top government officials, have more prestige and status than all other citizens.

The children who apply to the schools must be ten years old, be fine athletes, and have good academic records. They need not have had previous dance training but they must show exceptional aptitude for the dance. They must have a sense of rhythm and balance, musicality, and good coordination. In addition they must have good lungs and be in excellent physical condition. Finally they must appear to the doctors and teachers who examine them, to have a promise of beauty; as far as can be tested, it must seem that they will not grow up to be too tall, too short, too big, or need glasses in order to perform.

At entrance examinations there are many people watching, and sometimes movie and television cameramen take pictures. Even before they are accepted, the students are experiencing the strain of being in the public eye. Of all the students who apply for entrance, only about one in thirty is accepted. These enter at the age of ten and most

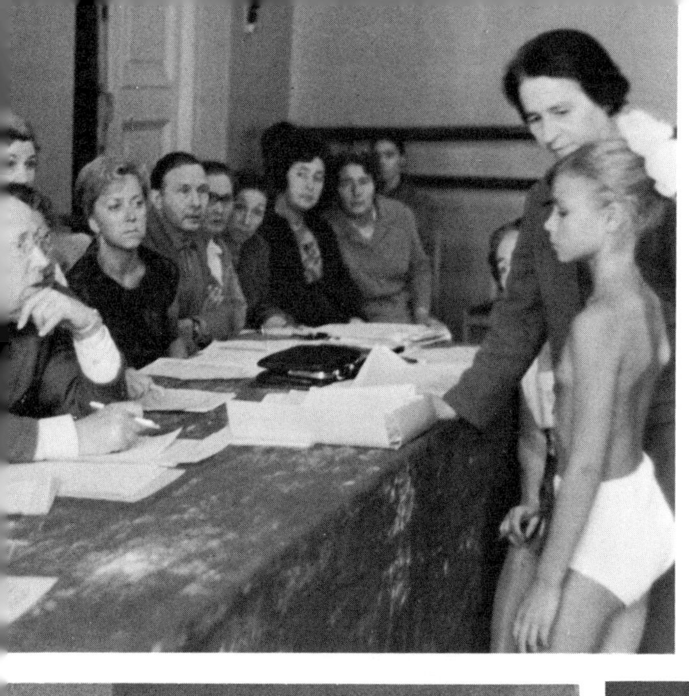

stay the full eight years. It is usually apparent within the first two years that a few are not going to make good dancers. These leave, and a second smaller group is accepted at the age of twelve to replace them. Only very special children are admitted after twelve. Scouts from the Kirov and Bolshoi schools go all over the country, and if they find an extraordinarily talented youngster in another school or amateur group, they take him. Nureyev was already "old," seventeen, when he was accepted into the Kirov School. Marina Leonova was discovered at fourteen in an amateur ballet club run for the children of workers in a Moscow steel factory where her father was a toolmaker. She was brought to the Bolshoi School.

For those lucky enough to be accepted, school begins September first; and it is traditional in Russia at the beginning of the school year and when returning from winter and spring holidays for the students to bring flowers to their teachers. About half the students are boys and half girls.

For all of them, school is free and, in fact, many of the most able students also receive stipends; their parents are actually paid to allow their children to attend ballet school. In the Bolshoi School there are six hundred and fifty students, about three hundred and fifty of them boarders, who come not only from all over the Soviet Union but from all over the world. The seven million dollar building is ultra-modern (one of the very few air-conditioned buildings in Moscow) and students get everything at no charge: books, practice clothes, at least four pairs of ballet shoes per month, and eventually costumes.

Because ballet is so important in Russia, there is no lack of money for all of this. The annual budget of the Bolshoi School is nearly two million dollars, and this is just to cover the cost of teachers and staff and to house and feed the students. The school receives extra funds for new choreographies, specially commissioned music, stage sets, costumes, and for trips abroad to student competitions, where the Russian students almost invariably capture the top prizes.

Entering students must adjust to the very strict discipline of the school. They must stand when an adult enters a classroom and must make a *révérence* to any adult entering or leaving a class. The children have little free time during the day, and the younger ones are forbidden to watch the classes of older students. Nevertheless breaches of discipline are not unknown. Although in most American schools children can't wait to leave the moment school is out, in ballet school in Russia, when the school day is finished, youngsters often sneak a look at the ad-

vanced classes to try to learn a little more. And sometimes in a class they obey an irresistible urge to whisper a secret or to giggle.

Ballet school students are required to take the same scholastic subjects as all other Russian children: history, geography, French, drawing, geometry, algebra, physics, biology, anatomy, chemistry, and, of course, Russian language and literature. These academic subjects are fitted into a schedule that also includes three to four-and-a-half hours of dancing classes a day, plus music, breathing, acting, history of the dance, and art history. Classes begin at nine and end at six—a long day.

If a student's report card reflects weakness in any subject, extra study and tutoring are required until that subject is improved. Each student gets a great deal of individual attention because academic classes never have more than thirty pupils. In the Bolshoi School there are two

hundred teachers for six hundred and fifty students. Both boarders and day students are encouraged to use the school library in order to increase their knowledge and understanding.

The state gives the schools enough money to hire the best possible teachers in each speciality. At the Bolshoi School, actors from the famous Moscow Art Theatre are brought in to teach students the art of acting. There are also lectures by famous writers, musicians, composers, painters, and choreographers, including some from other countries.

The students must perfect themselves in so many diverse subjects because ballet is an art that includes music and color and design and architecture and sculpture and light and drama as well as dance, so its students need to know the other arts. Also, most ballets in Russia are not abstract, but are about people and their motives and passions. In order effectively to portray people, either in dancing or in choreography, students must know history and biography and all the disciplines that lead to a knowledge of human nature and an understanding of the many varied aspects of the human enterprise.

But the main business of a ballet school is to teach dancing. And that is what the children most want to learn. From the very beginning instruction is intense and individual. There are seldom more than ten pupils in any ballet class.

First year students begin at the barre, a rail along the wall they grasp for balance. Here they learn the five classical ballet positions and certain long-established exercises and steps, including: *pliés*, *battements*, *ronds de jambe*, and *relevés*.

Some work is actually done behind the barre, because *pliés* must be done with the back straight, and behind the barre it's impossible to get down and up unless the back is straight. In Russia, as all over the world, ballet terminology is French because ballet was formalized in France under Louis XIV.

After working at the barre, the students proceed to the more advanced *center work*. It is many months, even years, before the girls move from demi-toe to full toe, when they are allowed to wear toe shoes. When that time

comes, they will have mastered the five basic positions and all of the elementary and many advanced steps. And this means a great deal of work. There are no short cuts in the ballet—no substitutes for hours and hours of practice.

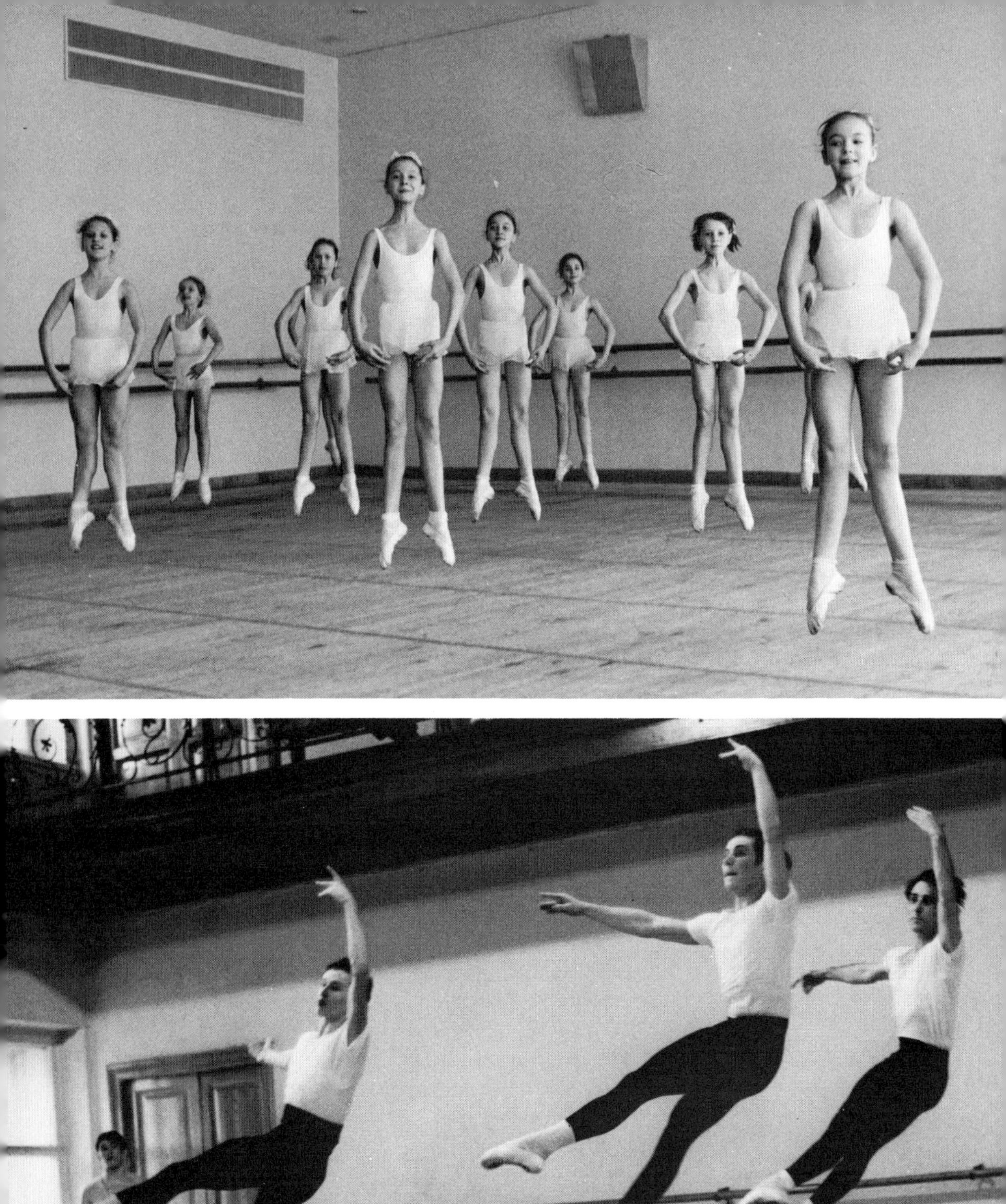

The boys must perfect the same simple and advanced steps before they are allowed to practice the great leaps and *cabrioles* for which Russian male dancers are famous.

Every movement of body, legs, arms, even fingers and eyes, is watched and corrected by the many teachers, most of whom are themselves former dancers. It is very difficult for the children to learn to accept the constant criticism, but it is necessary in order that they may learn and improve.

Perhaps even more difficult than accepting criticism, since the children at the school want so much to succeed, is hearing another child of the same age praised or seeing that he or she is clearly more talented. Even though most

ballets require a *corps de ballet* as well as star performers, each child wants to grow up to be a star and not merely a member of the *corps de ballet*. In both schools' fiercely competitive climate, it is hard for the students not to be envious of a classmate who dances better, even though all students are constantly reminded that some children develop later than others and that occasionally brilliant students have, in later years, not lived up to their early promise.

As the youngsters learn more and more and become used to the strict and disciplined atmosphere of the school, they feel more at home, more relaxed, more confident. But still a word of praise from the teacher for a step exceptionally well executed makes any one of them feel gloriously happy.

On the other hand, if after weeks and weeks of practice and of trying as hard as possible, a certain step still is not mastered, it can be heartbreaking. To an audience, ballet seems a beautiful, graceful, easy thing; but every student and dancer knows that the one constant of ballet is sweat. Endless practice, constant repetition, and exceptional talent may make a dance *look* easy; but the easier a dancer makes a role look, the more surely it is the result of long and sweaty work.

There are only ten minutes between classes so the students are always rushing from one class to another, especially when they have to change clothes between them. Much of the time the students are covered in thick sweaters and woolly leg warmers because they are often per-

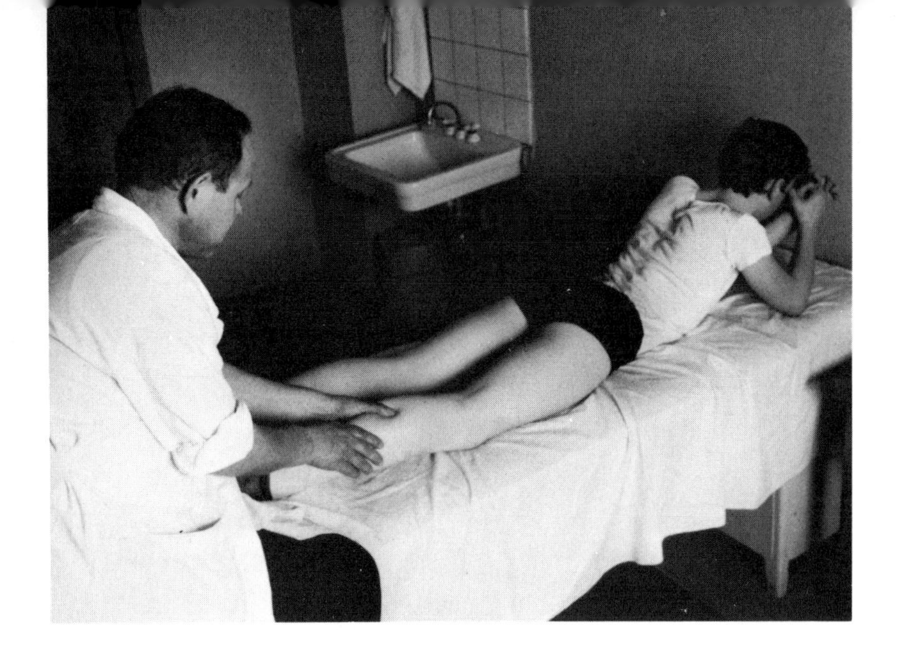

spiring and one of a dancer's chief fears is a cramped muscle caused by a sudden chill.

With such strenuous demands being made on the students' bodies, it is necessary to have right in the school not only therapists and masseurs, but also the latest scientific apparatuses to relieve pulled muscles and strained joints. The doctors who are always at the school are con-

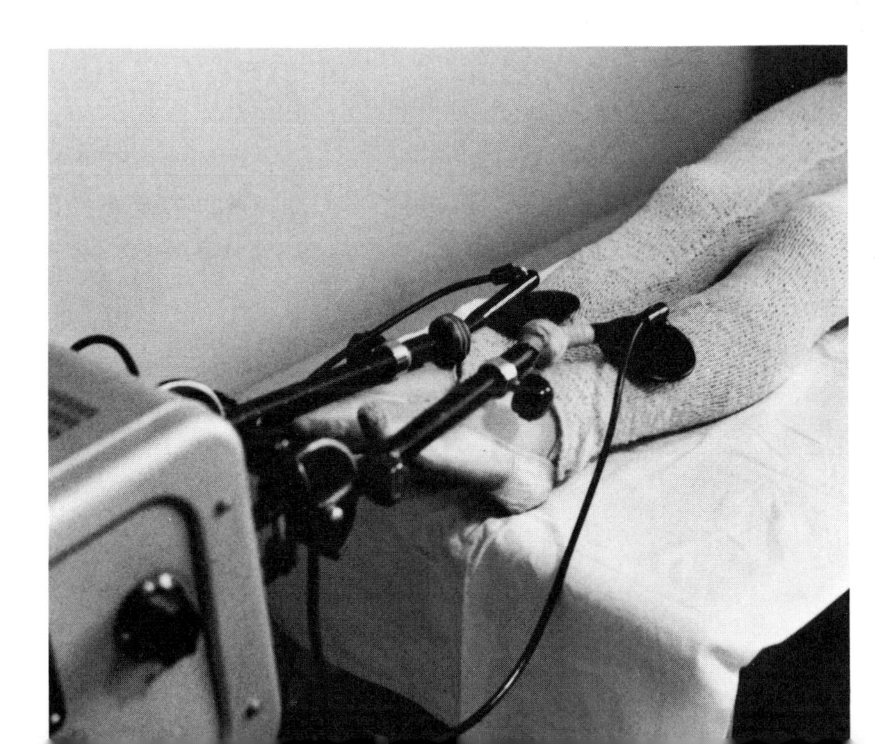

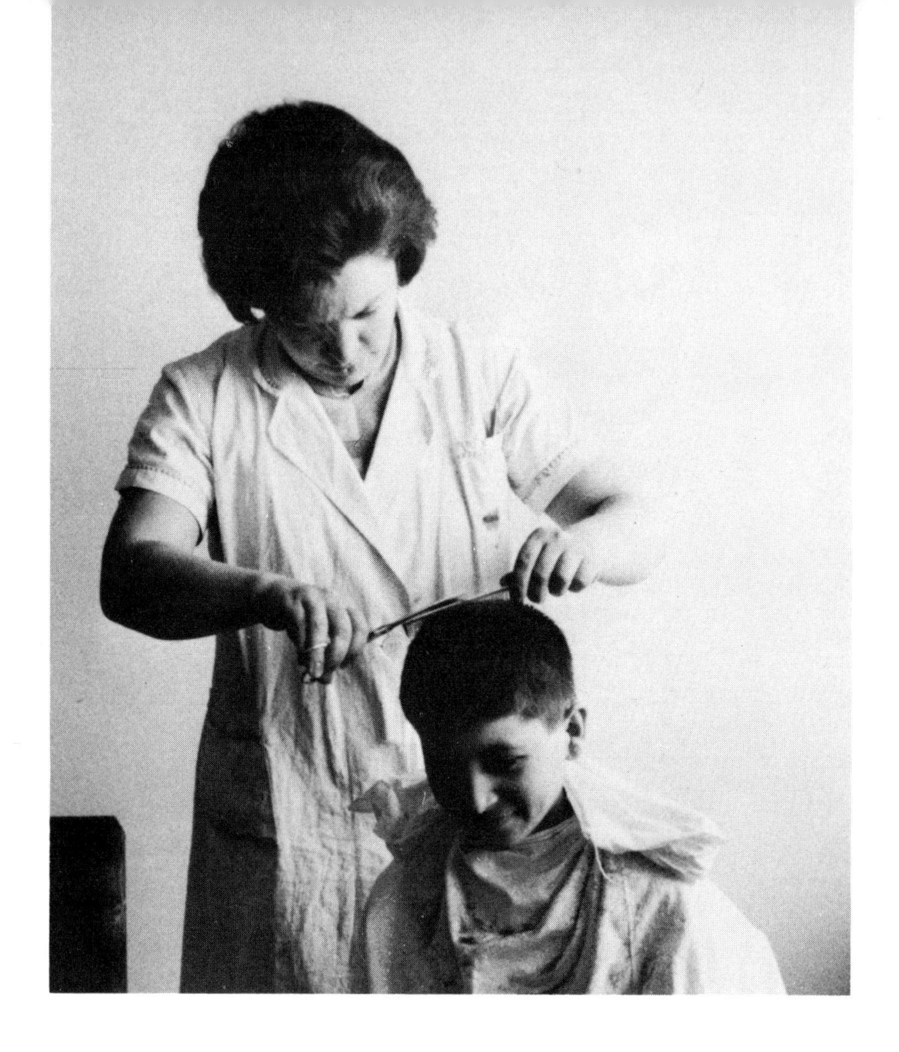

stantly checking the students to be sure they are in good physical condition, and there is also a resident dentist.

The school tries to have absolutely everything the students need, including a lady barber for the boys and a hairdresser for the girls. The hairdresser both gives permanents and teaches the girls how to do it for themselves. There is a laundry, but the pupils must wash their own practice clothes and socks and underwear every day.

Food is very important in the lives of ballet students. They must eat enough of the proper foods to give them energy and build their muscles, but not the kinds of foods that will make them fat. In the school cafeteria, dietitians and cooks see to it that the food is the right kind and has enough variety. Ballet students are forbidden to smoke or drink wine.

Proper relaxation is an absolute necessity for children under so much stress, and during the long school days (five and a half days a week) the children's schedules are arranged to alternate mental and physical activities.

Despite all the energy they expend in dance classes during the day, the students still have enough left for sports—basketball, soccer, gymnastics, and swimming. There are, however, no team sports, only informal games.

There is a free rest home where students may go for their winter holiday (January 10 to 20) and for spring vacation (the last week in March). Here they may ski and go sledding, but they are not allowed to ice-skate because it develops the wrong muscles.

At other times the pupils go on tours of the city. At museums they learn about their history and about beauty in many forms. At concerts and theaters and the circus they come to understand more about other performing arts and therefore more about their own. Such trips, beside enriching their experience and taste, provide relaxation and pleasure.

Boarding students are given time in the evening for both recreation and homework. They may play chess, shoot pool, watch television, knit, embroider, read or write a letter home.

There are always moments though when the best recreation is not doing something but doing nothing, just being alone and staring out of the window—daydreaming about the future, remembering home, or thinking of somebody one loves.

Many students are thousands of miles from home so getting letters is important. The youngest children are especially likely to be homesick; and if a letter from home doesn't come, or, if they feel they are not doing as well as they should in their dance classes, it falls to the House Mother to console them.

The House Mother also has disciplinary duties. A young man who plays hockey in the halls and later that same night is caught shooting a water pistol gets a severe talking to. Despite the strict discipline, snowball fights, pigtail pulling, teasing, name calling, hiding clothes or books, tying a friend's clothes in knots, and other forms of mischief are not unknown; punishment is sure and swift for anyone who is caught.

For the youngest students "lights out" is at nine, but the older ones may stay up until eleven. Even the eighteen-year-old boarders, however, must have written permission to go out in the evening and must be back in the dormitory by eleven. Over the weekend the rules are relaxed somewhat, and the latest popular dances from the West often replace Tchaikovsky and the classical ballet. School ends June first for the younger students and two weeks later for the older ones, and they are all free to rest until September.

But wherever students of either school are, whatever their age and whether it is winter or summer, their minds are most apt to be filled with dancing. And much of the time, in class and out, they are thinking not just of dancing but of performing.

In geography class they may look at the map and dream about the day when their art will take them all over the world on tour. The students are frequently told that when they tour with a ballet, they will be serving as cultural ambassadors of their country.

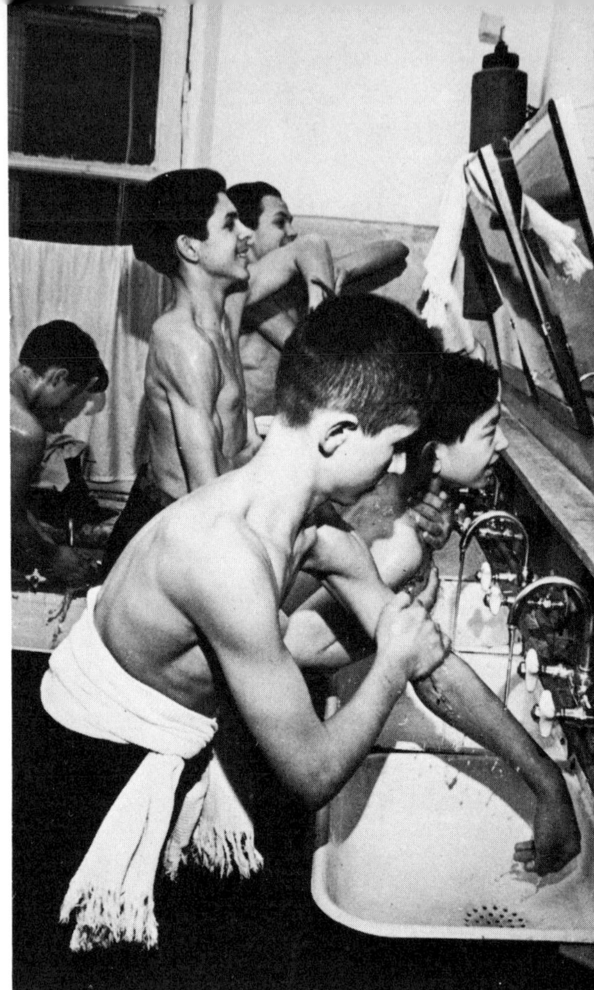

At the classes in makeup they anticipate the variety of roles that may someday be theirs. They learn to make themselves look older or younger, happy or sad, saintly or wicked. For some roles, the children learn, they may have to wear body makeup, which can sometimes be very difficult to remove, especially in a small, backstage dressing room, and they are taught not only how to put it on, but how to take it off.

In the dance classes themselves, students are not only preparing their muscles for the demands of difficult roles and learning intricate dance patterns, but are also preparing for the stage on which they will eventually perform. In Russia as in Europe, dancers use resin on their shoes to keep from slipping but do not spread resin on the floor, as dancers do in America. Instead, they sprinkle water over the floor, and each student in class takes his or her turn with the watering can. Also the stages in Russia, as in Europe, are not flat as they are in America: they are raked downward from back to front so that the audience can better see the dancers' feet. For this reason all the floors in the practice rooms are also raked in order that the students may become used to dancing on a slanted surface.

Critics all over the world have marvelled at what great partners the male Russian dancers are. One reason for this is that the boys and girls in Russian ballet schools practice dancing together at an earlier age than in most countries. In this way they get used to duet dancing and to the lifts that are such an exciting and spectacular part of ballet.

Since performing will be so great a part of the students' lives once they have graduated, it is also made a large part of their lives in school. The Bolshoi School has a four hundred seat theater of its own. This theater is fully lighted and equipped, and there students not only practice and rehearse but also put on full productions, both of the great classical ballets and of ballets written and choreographed specially for them. For these they have their own sets and costumes. The public may attend these performances; and by being in them, students become used to an audience as well as to the lights and backstage problems of a theater.

In addition to performances at school, the students perform regularly in the Kirov or the Bolshoi theaters, both in the ballets that require children—including *Nutcracker*, *Romeo and Juliet*, *Don Quixote*, and *Sleeping Beauty*—and in opera productions that require children—like *Carmen*, *Faust*, *Aïda*, and *Pique Dame*. When the Kirov and Bolshoi ballet companies are away on tour, the best students replace the *corps de ballet* in the theaters; and of course, when there are leading roles for children in ballets (as in *Nutcracker*), these are taken by top students from the schools.

Very rarely too, students may dance leading adult roles even before graduating from school. Two great Russian ballerinas of today, Besmertnova and Sorokina, for example, gave indication when they were still little girls that they would be superb dancers; and both, before graduating, were dancing the lead in *Chopiniana* in the Bolshoi Company. But these are rare exceptions. For most students there is only the agonizingly slow and difficult, step by step training period over many years.

But in the school there is always something going on so exciting that the hard work and the aches seem worth it and the possibilities for the future seem glorious. A Russian or foreign film maker or television crew may come and take movies of the classes or of a student performance, and sometimes the students are allowed to peer through the camera to see how the film will look. Or a producer from the Russian film industry may come looking for an exceptionally talented and beautiful child to borrow for a movie role.

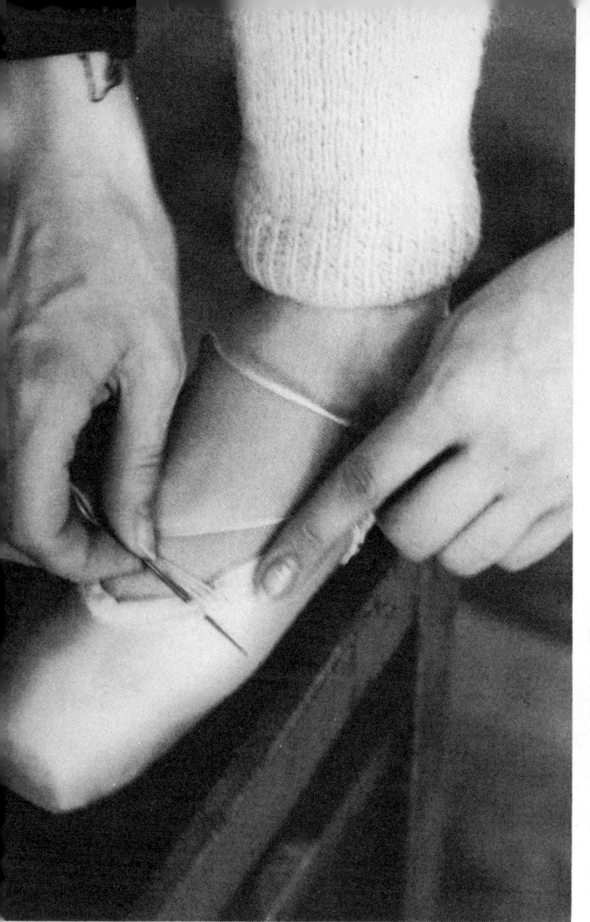

Nevertheless, in spite of all the preparation and all the anticipation, the last moments before going on to the great Bolshoi stage for the first time are nervous ones for any new dancer.

Russian toe shoes are cut lower than those in the West, so the girls must stitch across the instep of each shoe for greater support.

The Russians also take no chances with hooks and eyes; before each performance, each student is sewn into his or her costume.

Finally there are last minute instructions from the Directress, which help the dancer forget her stage fright. Sofia Nikolaievna Golovkina, head of the Bolshoi School, was herself a great ballerina. She still serves her art, now that she can no longer perform, by passing on her knowledge to students.

The performers are always relieved when any performance is over, and thrilled to hear the applause. It is the custom in Russia for the performers also to applaud the audience.

ОЛЬШОЙ ТЕАТР СССР

ТРАВИАТА

1

ЦВЕТИК-СЕМИЦВЕТИК

2

ВЕСНА СВЯЩЕННАЯ

КАРМЕН-СЮИТА

ЩЕЛКУНЧИК

А

ЧИО-ЧИО-САН

6

ОПТИМИСТИЧЕСКАЯ ТРАГЕДИЯ

Ь

ЦИРЮЛЬНИК

When the pupils are not performing themselves, they attend performances three or four nights a week, watching sometimes from out front and sometimes from backstage, absorbing the beauty and magic of the theater and coming to feel at home in the artistic atmosphere in which they will be spending most of their lives. They study the posters of each week's performances to see which stars are dancing which roles, much as children in the West who follow baseball or football keep track of their favorite players. At the same time these ballet students dream of that future day when their own names will appear on the posters.

After seeing a performance, whether of ballet or theater or symphony, the students go back to school and discuss it: What was good? What was poor? What was new to them? What could have been done differently or better? Seeing the best, they get used to the best and so develop high standards. Often they see in the evening something they have studied as "history of art" during the day, and so they come to realize that they will soon be part of the flow of art history.

The blue and gold interior of the Maryinsky Theatre where the Kirov performs is one of the most beautiful in the world, an enchanted fairyland place; and the Bolshoi Theatre at night seems a magical temple of art, worth all the hard work and sore muscles and heartaches required of those who would perform there.

Finally after years of hard work, after many student performances and perhaps some performances on the stages of the great theaters themselves comes the final test, the state examinations. To prepare for these takes not only regular classes, but also many hours of special individual classes and many more hours of rehearsing all alone. Many times a day the muscle aching, bone tiring work makes a pupil feel too exhausted to go on. But a moment's rest, a soft drink, a bit of fruit, or just a word of praise is enough to make him go on. And go on he must, regardless of aching knee or calf or ankle, if he is to learn all he must before the final state examinations.

After the state examinations, the student will learn where he or she will go next: to one of the two greatest companies, the Kirov or the Bolshoi, as a soloist or a member of the *corps de ballet;* as a performer to a lesser theater in Moscow or Leningrad or to one of the thirty other opera and ballet houses in the country; or to teach in one of the many ballet schools. Or perhaps the student will not be a ballet dancer, strictly speaking, at all. Classes are given at both schools in folk dancing, Spanish dancing, and a few in modern dancing.

The boy or girl who hasn't the ability to perform classical ballet, may be especially good at folk dancing and, if so, on graduation may go on to stardom in the folk dance company of Igor Moiseyev. Or if a student has a particular genius for acting, he or she may end up playing some of the character parts in the ballets at the Kirov or Bolshoi; these are not the very top leading roles, but are important and well-known principal parts. And a very few graduates have left the ballet to go into theater or the movies.

Whether the child who began his intensive study of the dance at the age of ten—an age when he could hardly know all of the career choices open to him and could not even know all of his own interests and talents—might have been happier had he waited and chosen an entirely different career, is, of course, impossible to determine. Any stu-

dent who wants to, may leave one of the specialized ballet schools to go to a regular academic school, but none has ever chosen to do so. Once they are in the terribly competitive atmosphere, they become infected with the fever of the art, and the very few who leave do so not by their own choice but only for reasons of health, discipline, or lack of talent.

Had the child been forced to wait until a later age before choosing a career, he or she might have decided instead to become a scientist or poet or doctor, and so in theory this Russian system of early specialization may well deprive the nation of some great scientists or poets or doctors. But in practice that system also produces the best ballet dancers in the world.

After the state examinations, there remains only the Graduation Performance. There, before an audience of state officials, foreign dignitaries, teachers and fellow students, and, of course, proud parents and friends, each boy and girl dances the best role of which he is capable after his long years of training. This is his valedictory to student life.

The dance companies the young dancers are then ready to join are the world's greatest in traditional and classical dance, though not in modern and abstract dance. Now both the Bolshoi and the Kirov are putting more effort into this area, but only the future will tell how successful they may be. Classical ballet is wholly apolitical and, therefore, not subject to censorship and the suppression of artistic freedom, which more modern dance might encounter, as have writing and painting in the Soviet Union.

Once they join a dance company, the graduates are performers, practicing as professionals the art of which they were so long students. There will still be years of daily classes, there will be endless rehearsals, and the learning of new roles and the polishing of old ones. But at last they have arrived at their long sought goal—they are artists of the Russian ballet.